The Exercises of
St Ignatius Loyola
and
Traditions of the East

Inigo Text Series: 14

The Exercises of St Ignatius Loyola and Traditions of the East

Javier Melloni, S.J.

Translated by
Michael Kirwan, S.J.

First published in 2013
jointly by

Gracewing 　　　　　　　Inigo Enterprises
2 Southern Avenue 　　　Links View, Traps Lane
Leominster 　　　and　　New Malden
Herefordshire 　　　　　Surrey KT3 4RY
HR6 0QF

*'The expense is reckoned; the enterprise is begun.
It is of God . . .'*

All rights reserved. No part of this publication may be reproduced, stored in a retrieval system, or transmitted in any form, or by any means, electronic, mechanical, photocopying, recording or otherwise, without the written permission of the publisher.

© 2013 Javier Melloni, S.J.

The right of Javier Melloni to be identified as the author of this work has been asserted in accordance with the Copyright, Designs and Patents Act, 1988.

ISBN 978 085244 769 7

Typesetting by
Action Publishing Technology Ltd, Gloucester GL1 5SR

CONTENTS

Foreword	vii
Introduction	1
1. Elements	5
2. Dynamisms	
2.1 The Spiritual Exercises and Yoga	21
The *Yoga Sutras*	22
The Three Yogas of the Bhagavad Gita	28
The *Yoga Karma* or the Yoga of Action	29
The *Bhakti Yoga* or the Yoga of Devotion	31
The *Jnana Yoga* or the Yoga of Knowledge	33
2.2 The Spiritual Exercises and Zen	37
2.3 Development of Some Points	51
a. Presence and absence of images and discursive thought	51
b. On the historical dimension	52
c. Effort and grace	53
d. Extinction of the ego and decentring	55
e. Presence and absence of a divine 'Thou'	56
f. In search of the Absolute	58
Conclusions	60
Further Reading	65

FOREWORD

The main purpose of this Foreword is to help the reader to appreciate some of the implications of the title Javier Melloni has given his book: *The Exercises of St Ignatius Loyola and Traditions of the East*. It is important to do this before plunging into the rest of the book.

It is also important for the reader to give this first initiative the fullest quality of attentive time; even if this is as little as fifteen minutes.

The title is prosaic, but it expresses as exactly as any words can the author's *key insight*: to indicate integrations we have scarcely begun to recognise; encouraging the *key action*: to let ourselves be interrogated and enriched by the contributions of other religious traditions; following the *key principle*: all originate in the same Fount and return to it through the same paradoxes of God or the ultimate reality; expressed in the *key sentence*: fullness spills over into donation: that is, neither by emptying of the self nor by substituting another self, but a balancing of each reaching beyond both.

Billy Hewett SJ
Director, Inigo Enterprises

Introduction

In these pages we will compare three spiritual pathways which underlie the traditions of three different religions: the Spiritual Exercises of St Ignatius, linked with Christianity; Yoga, which proceeds from Hinduism; and Zen, originating from the womb of Buddhism. With an understanding of these three ways we place ourselves at the heart of their respective traditions, as suggested by the Latin saying: *Lex orandi, lex credendi*, that is to say, prayer – and by extension, every spiritual practice – is the reflection of a mode of belief, just as every belief is configured to the extent to which it is prayed.

We will seek to present these three ways with a double purpose: to show the specific elements of each one, as well as their common or convergent points. Only if we do not confuse them can we recognise both the difficulty and the richness to be found in placing them in relation with one another. To integrate is not the same as to mix up.

Above all, what certainly unites the three ways is that they are not speculative, but initiatory or mystagogical. Their objective is the transformation of the person who undertakes them, to admit that person into the experience of the Absolute. What remains to be seen is in what direction and by what means, because each one belongs in a wider framework, namely the presuppositions of its own religion. Perhaps the most extreme polarity is between Christianity and Buddhism. It has been said that Christianity is characterised as essentially *agapaic*, a religion of love (*agape*), while Buddhism is essentially gnostic (*prajna*), a religion of consciousness.[1] Between both, we position Hinduism, in the sense that it contains devotional elements (*bhakti*) and cognitive ones (*jnana*), combined differently according to the various schools.[2] This intermediate position of Hinduism corresponds to its conception of the divine: if Christianity is at the extreme of the personification of God and Buddhism at the opposite extreme, of impersonification, Hinduism, in its multiple currents and schools, is situated between the two.

Still by way of introduction, it will be worthwhile to have a brief presentation of the three spiritual practices under consideration.

The Spiritual Exercises of Ignatius (written between 1522 and 1548) are a very representative example of Catholic Christianity. Although they were elaborated by one individual, they echo the practice of the preceding thousand years.[3] By Catholic Christianity I understand that branch of Christianity grounded in the mysticism of the following of Christ. In speaking of the following of Christ I refer to two things: on the one hand, to the centrality of the figure of Jesus, as a concrete divine-human presence, an object of love and devotion, and on the other, to the personal and historical character of this following: that each person who comes into contact with Jesus, in a unique and unrepeatable manner, makes possible a transformation through following him. The reality of the Exercises is rooted in the principle of

---

[1] Cf. Aloysius Pieris, *Love Meets Wisdom. A Christian Experience of Buddhism*. Orbis Books, Maryknoll, New York, 1988.

[2] The current *bhaktica* or devotional element conceives of God as a being with a personal existence (*Brigaha*), while the current *jnana* conceives of him as an impersonal Being, characterised as *Sat* (Truth), *Chi* (Conscience) and *Ananda* (happiness).

[3] See number 5 of this Series: Javier Melloni, *The Exercises of St Ignatius Loyola in the Western Tradition*, Gracewing & Inigo Enterprises, 2000.

personalisation, and in the discernment of how this following makes itself concrete in history.

Yoga is one of the six great systems (*darshanas*, 'points of view') of Hinduism.[4] It offers an overwhelming variety of schools and sub-schools: Hatha Yoga (yoga of postures), Raja Yoga (of meditation), Tantra Yoga (of the activation of energies), Kriya Yoga (of combined action), etc. *Yoga* literally means 'union',[5] both because it seeks the unification of the body, psychically, mentally and spiritually, and to unite with the Absolute being (Brahman, Para-Atman, Sat-Chit-Ananda ... according to the currents).

Zen is a Japanese term which means 'meditation'. It derives from *ch'an*, a Chinese word which in turn derives from the Sanskrit *dhyana*. It belongs to the Mahayana branch of Buddhism (the 'Great Vehicle'), the most speculative and elaborate of the three great branches of Buddhism. Mahayana extended through the whole of China from the beginning of the third century AD, and then to Japan. The two other great branches of Buddhism are: Hinayana ('Small Vehicle'), also known by the name of Theravada ('of the Ancients', as it sees itself closest to the teaching of Buddha), and Vajrayan, or Buddhism 'of the ray' or 'the diamond', identified with Tibetan Buddhism, which is marked by the shamanic substratum which existed before the arrival of Buddhism in Tibet (from the eighth century AD). Zen did not come to Japan until the twelfth century, enriched by elements of Chinese Taoism. The influence of this stream

---

[4] The other five systems are: *Samkya*, with a metaphysical character; *Vaisshesika*, cosmological; *Nyaya*, logical; *Purvamimansa*, of a more exegetical character, with reference to the sacred texts of the Vedas; and the *Uttararamimansa* or *Vedanta*, of great metaphysical and mystical profundity, to which belong the *Upanishads*.

[5] It derives from the Sanskrit root, 'yuj', from which comes yoke, meaning 'someone who maintains unity'.

can be perceived in features such as the principle of 'non-action' (*wu wei*) and in the different shades of emptiness, which, on the other hand, are already present in Buddhism.

This brief introduction has situated each of the three spiritual practices within its own tradition.

In order to establish a comparison between them, we will proceed in three parts: first, I will present the fundamental features of each pathway. In spite of its fragmentary and at times excessively synthetic character, this section is indispensable for establishing the basic terms of each stream. In a second section I will compare their dynamics, pointing out the divergent and convergent points. Then I will discuss some basic elements of the spiritual experience in order to see how they are tackled in each pathway, and I shall conclude with a reflection upon the fitness of each practice, with attention to each person in their concrete moment.

1. ELEMENTS

ELEMENTS	SPIRITUAL EXERCISES	YOGA	ZEN
1. SUBJECTS OF THE PROCESS	- I and Thou	- I and Thou	- I and Thou
2. FOCUS	- following of and identification with Christ	- Non-duality between *atman-*Brahman	- *Sunyata* ('emptyness')
3. ULTIMATE GOAL	- Christification	- *moksha* ('liberation')	- *Nirvana* ('extinction') - buddhic nature
4. SPECIFIC PURPOSE	- to search the will of God	- to reach *samadhi* ('absorption')	- To reach *satori* ('enlightenment')
5. ANTHRO-POLOGICAL VEHICLES	- memory - understanding - will, senses, affections, - desires	- body - breathing - seven *chakras*	- posture - breathing - *hara*
6. PRACTICES	- meditations - contemplations - application of senses - examen of prayer	- *asanas* ('postures') - *pranayama* ('breathing exercises') - *dharana* ('concentration') - *dhyana* ('meditation')	- *Zazen* ('sitting into depth') - open eyes - awareness - *Seshin* ('meeting within the heart')
7. TOOLS	- Gospel passages - points for prayer	- breathing - mantras	- breathing - *koans*
8. DISPOSITION	- indifference - generosity	- *viraga* ('detachment') - determination	- *mu-shin* ('non-heart') - determination (*dai-funshi*)
9. OBSTACLES	- sins - disordered affections unconscious wounds - wrong images of God and of oneself - distractions	- *avidya* ('ignorance') - *Kama, raga* ('desires') - *vritti* ('perturbations of the thought') - *ahamkara* ('ego conscience')	- *avidya* ('ignorance') - *trishna* ('avidity') - *vritti* ('perturbations of the thought') - *makyo* ('hallucinations')
10. TYPES OF AWARENESS	- discernment - inner knowledge	- *viveka* ('discernment') - *anubhava* ('experimental knowledge') - *jnana* ('wisdom')	- awareness - *prajna* ('wisdom')
11. ACCOMPANIMENT	- meeting with the one who gives the Sp Ex	- *darshan* with the guru ('meeting the one who banishes darkness')	- *Dokusan* with the *roshi* (interview with the master)

1.1 THE SUBJECTS OF THE PROCESS

It is convenient to begin by clarifying what are the subjects – human and divine – to emerge from the encounter which has been initiated, since their conception corresponds to very different anthropological and theological models.

The Exercises are fundamentally constructed on the basis of the relation between the *I* of the exercitant and the *Thou* of God. This relation will be displaced on the journey, to the point of discovering that the most real 'I' is that of God: 'I am who I am' (Ex 3:14), while the human 'I' is the you which God causes to be. The relation 'I-Thou' (or 'Thou-I') is constitutive, not only of the Ignatian Exercises, but of Christianity. Christianity is a religion of relation, which has its roots in the biblical experience: God who is moved to tenderness on account of the weakness of his people, with whom he also pleads and calls to be faithful. The solicitude of God of the Old Testament reaches its critical point in Jesus Christ, where God shows his face. The experience of the Exercises, insofar as it participates in the Christian religious universe, is inconceivable without the relational character of the faith.

This is not so in the framework of Hinduism, still less in Buddhism. Although Hinduism has many schools, and is also aware of the relational and affective dimension (*bhaktica*) with Brahman in numerous manifestations (Vishnu, Rama, Krishna, Shiva . . .), the characteristic of the way of Yoga is the interiorisation of divine Being and experience of the *advatic* relation which exists between the individual 'I' (*atman*) and the Total Being (Brahman or Paratman). *Advaitism*, although only one of the three great interpretive schools of vedantic Hindusim,[6] is the

---

[6] The other two schools are: Visishtadvaita (qualified non-duality), defended by Ramanuja (1055–1137), and Dvaita, or dualist, defended by Madhva (1199–1278).

most significant. It conceives of the relation between the individual I and the Divine Being as neither dualist nor monist: that is to say, that there is neither separation nor absorption on the part of either of the two poles. The experience of *advaita* is precisely the end of Yoga, in which, without ceasing to have an 'i' and a Thou (or an 'I' and a 'thou'), this relation is transcended in a maximum of community and of fullness.

In Buddhism, the *advaitic* posture is even more radicalised, because it prescinds from all personalisation, both of the subject who meditates and the Absolute Reality over which he or she meditates. From the beginning the subject seeks to eliminate all consciousness of ego which allows the formation of thinking that some 'I' exists. And if there is no 'I', neither is there a 'Thou' to refer to, rather a unique Reality to which individual consciousness is called to open itself, until all self-reference has disappeared. This Reality, which transcends individualities, is pure emptiness (*sunyata*), but not a vacuous emptiness, rather a full emptiness, the womb of all the forms, the origin and return of all particular manifestations, among which is the 'I' which meditates.

1.2–1.3 FOCUS AND ULTIMATE GOAL OF EACH WAY

The Exercises unfold in the ambit of the following of Christ, with the object of achieving the greatest possible identification with him. This identification is called 'christification', although it is not formulated as such by Ignatius. What is explicitly mentioned in the Exercises is the expression 'salvation of the soul'. (EE 23) What saves the soul is the 'praise, reverence and service of God our Lord' (23), which Jesus Christ fully realised. Salvation and christification are two ways of speaking of the same thing: of the plenitude of life in God. In Yoga, on the other hand, an attempt is made to achieve a state of liberation (*moksha*) in which the dualism between the *atman* – the individual spirit – and *Brahman*, the Supreme being from whom everything arises, without ceasing to be Him, is transcended. In Zen, one moves into Emptiness (*sunyata*) in order to arrive at awakening of 'buddha-ness', or buddhic nature, where *Nirvana* is achieved. In Mahayana Buddhism 'buddha-ness' is the ultimate essence of the human being, just as christification – or divine filiation – denotes the destiny of the human being in Christianity.

1.4 THE SPECIFIC PURPOSE OF EACH WAY

The Exercises claim to 'seek and discover the divine will in the disposition of one's life for the salvation of souls'. (EE 1.4) Christification, to which we referred above, takes place through the quest for, and the handing over to, the will of God one's own life. It will imply learning two types of knowledge: the capacity to discern that will, and to go deeply into the 'internal knowledge' of Christ. (EE 104)

On the other hand, what Yoga seeks is a state of absorption in the non-duality called *samadhi*. This highpoint constitutes the eighth stage of a progression we shall see later on. The different yogic exercises seek to purify the obstacles which impede the individual being from merging itself with the Absolute.

In the practice of Zen there is an attempt to achieve *satori*, whose characteristics are distinct from the Hindu *samadhi*: it does not seek to achieve a state of absorption, but of lucidity and of wakefulness. *Satori* signifies precisely this: 'illumination', 'awakening'. What Zen intends is that the practitioner opens themself to the totality of the Real, transcending the egocentric captivity of the 'I'. For this reason, Zen meditation, in contrast to the yogic meditation, is practiced with half-open eyes. This is due to the difference of intentions: yoga seeks *samadhi* ('absorption') for which the eyes have to be preserved from all contact with the exterior; by contrast, to the extent that Zen seeks *satori*, illumination, it is important to stay awake.

1.5 THE ANTHROPOLOGICAL VEHICLES

In general terms, we may say that the Ignatian Exercises are to be read among the positive ways, while Zen is situated among the negative ways. Between both are the practices of Yoga, combining both elements. The positive ways are those which convoke the various psychical dimensions of the human being in order to accede to what is beyond them, while the negative ways are those which from the beginning seek to annul all mental and affective activity. The Ignatian Exercises activate and put into play all the human capacities, which in the scholastic vocabulary of the time were identified as the memory, the understanding and the will. Under the term 'will' is included affections and desires, that is to say the dynamisms which move and determine human love. It is intended that in the course of the journey all those forces are liberated and gathered into the following of Jesus and of the values of the Kingdom, above all, poverty and humility. (EE 98, 136–147) At the same time, use of the senses is activated, through the practice of certain penances and imaginative exercises, such as the *Application of the Senses*. (EE 121–125) Although there is some mention of bodily postures in the Annotations (EE 75–76), and of use of breathing in the third method of prayer (EE 258), they are relatively marginal to the wider picture.

Zen is the exact opposite, seeking to neutralise the mental and affective dimension in order to achieve emptiness. It considers that only thus can one arrive at another state of consciousness. Between both extremes we find the diverse schools of Yoga, which oscillate between the potential capacity of the faculties (*via positiva*) and their arrest (*via negativa*). Yoga and Zen both regard the body as the fundamental vehicle, although in different ways. In Yoga, the first to be worked on is the bodily disposition, by which the meditator can remain still for a long time in meditation. Hence the diverse postures (*asanas*). Even the breathing plays an important part as a preparatory step. Therefore when we speak of the organism, in Yoga one does not think solely of the physical body, but also of energy. In the anatomy of the energised body there are seven centres (*chakras*) in which this energy is situated. Each one of these *chakras* is related to diverse glands and organs of the body.

a. *Muladhara*, situated at the base of the spinal column, and has to be regarded as the foundation, base and roots of the person on earth.
b. *Svadistahana*, connected with the genital organs, and is related to the capacity to generate life, with physical desire, and with domination.
c. *Manipura*, situated in the solar plexus, and is seen as the emotions, fears, personality, and self-esteem.
d. *Anahata*, situated at the top of the heart, and has a relation with the sentiments, with the capacity to relate and to love, with compassion and pardon.
e. *Vishuddha*, situated in the stomach, has to be seen with the thyroid glands, and is related to the capacity for self-expression and creativity.
f. *Ajna*, situated in the forehead and is called the 'third eye', which is linked with the pinal gland and with

intuitive knowledge, with profound perception, and with wisdom.
g. *Sahasrara*, situated in the crown of the head, which opens onto the properly spiritual and transcendent dimension.

The exercises of Yoga seek to unify the energy which corresponds to each centre, gathering from above, but activating from below. The more inferior the *chakras*, the more dense and earthly their energy. The superior *chakras* correspond to more subtle and spiritual energies, but all are important, since all are constitutive of the human being.

In Zen, the centres of energy are concentrated in one, the *hara*, situated under the navel (between the second and third chakra of Yoga). In order to achieve its full expansion it is necessary to be aware of posture. So important is this, that it has been said that if Zen has any dogma at all, it is the position that must be maintained during meditation: a perfect positioning of the pelvis over the cushion; an erect spine, shoulders relaxed and held back, and the head slightly inclined from above, as if small threads were stretching from the crown.

1.6–1.7 PRACTICES AND SUPPORTS

In order to activate the affective memory, the intelligence and the desires, the Ignatian practice proposes a series of spiritual exercises, understood as 'every way of preparing and disposing the soul to rid itself of disordered affections (...) and to seek and discover the divine will'. (EE 1, 3–4) This variety takes into account diverse physical ambits: the way of eating and drinking (EE 83; 210–217), of sleeping (EE 73–74; 84); or relaxing (EE 1), of arranging one's surroundings, according to the theme which is being considered (EE 78–79; 206; 229), ... With everything, of primary importance are the mental exercises (meditations, considerations and contemplations), during which the specific material with which one is to work is presented, and whose content constitutes the guiding thread of the four Weeks. These are 'mental exercises' in two senses: in the first place, because they are not oral or vocal, insofar as they do not involve prayers spoken out loud, but are silent or interior. In the second place, the term 'mental' indicates that they are not significantly corporeal, but seek primarily to illumine the mind so as to accomplish a discernment, which has an undeniably 'mental' element. The support used are the passages from the Gospels. Although the small book of the Exercises does not propose texts from the Old Testament, in actual practice the psalms, texts from the prophets and other biblical passages are habitually used for meditations. On the other hand, at the end of each prayer and at the end of the day, an examen is proposed of how it has gone, in order to be conscious of the lived experience and its offer of conversion. This examination of conscience has been interpreted in recent years as an 'examination of consciousness',[7] in this way approximating to the practices of the East, which seek not so much to make an evaluation of the lived experience, but to maximise consciousness of the present moment.

In the practice of Yoga, on the other hand, there is a maximum reduction of the word and of mental activity in order to concentrate the attention solely on the body and on breathing. The first step consists of bodily postures (*asanas*), which serve as we have said to activate physically and energetically the separate organs and

---

[7] Cf. the famous article by George Ashenbrenner, 'Consciousness Examen', in *Review for Religious* 31 (1972), 14–21.

members, in such a way that the body can dispose itself through a long period of immobility without distractions or annoyances. The respiratory exercises continue (*pranayamas*), with the objective of centring the mind as well as energising the body. Then follow some concentration exercises, which can be summarised as two: visual (external images which are interiorised) and aural, through the repetition of a *mantra*. Mantra means literally 'instrument of control', which is identified with a specific sound, which varies in regard to the function of the state or disposition of the yogi. The mantra par excellence is AUM, 'a theophany reduced to the state of a phoneme', to use the expression of Mircea Eliade. This means the primordial sound of the universe, whose repetition allows entry into consonance with the whole of existence. Such are the fundamental supports of Yoga which facilitate uninterrupted meditation (*dhyana*) and afterwards *Samadhi* (transpersonal absorption).

In Zen, the fundamental practice is *zazen*, meditation, best translated as 'sitting in absorption'. During Zen retreats or *seshin* – a term which means 'encounter of the heart' – meditation is intensely practised, between five and ten hours daily, according to the grace of initiation, normally in thirty-minute segments interrupted by a slow walk (*kin-hin*). This walk carried out in the interior of the room serves to stimulate the blood circulation, which otherwise distracts the attention, which is now applied to a new activity: being conscious of the walking. With respect to the meditative practice, there are two great currents: the Soto school, also termed 'Zen of the peasant', which fundamentally uses breathing as a support. It proposes being simply seated (*shikantaza*), and to learn to detach oneself, allowing things to be what they are: 'When one is seated in tranquillity, the tree grows, the spring comes, and the flowers fall'. In contrast, the Rinzai school centres its practice in the 'great doubt', in the 'great determination' and in the 'great faith', and according to the preferred method the resolution of the *koan*, phrases or paradoxical stories which serve to alter the level of consciousness. The *koan* are not in an absolute sense riddles which need to be resolved mentally, but seek precisely the opposite: to interrupt the mental flow. In fact, the *koan* are resolved corporeally, that is to say, with the totality of one's being.[8]

1.8 DISPOSITION

Through the extent of the Exercises the aim is to achieve an attitude which is fundamental for being able to discern the will of God: indifference. Without it, there is no possible elucidation of one's life. Indifference is the liberty of heart which allows transparency of the love of God. What is opposed to this transparency is disordered affections. Together with indifference, it is required that the exercitant undertakes the Exercises with maximum generosity: 'It will be very profitable to enter them with great spirit and liberality'. (EE 5)

These two attitudes of indifference and of unconditional handing over to the practice are also present in the two other ways. In Yoga, the equivalent term to indifference is *viraga*, which can also be translated as impartiality or detachment. The yogi should overcome the disaffection of everything which is the cause of pain or pleasure, and seek the extinction of all self-centred perception in order to be attentive to the essential. On the other hand, the fifth observation of yoga (*niyama*) is the

---

[8] Cf. as an example J. K. Kadowaki on the *koan* of the raised finger of Gutei, in his work *Zen and the Bible*, Routledge & Kegan Paul, New York, 1980.

handing over to God (*Ishvara pranidhana*), which implies a determined and generous adhesion to the way which has begun.

In Zen it is a matter of achieving *mu-shin*, the 'non-heart'. As with the example of Ignatian indifference (or *apatheia* of the Desert Fathers), this expression can be misunderstood, insofar as it may be understood to mean insensitivity, an absence of fellow feeling and disengagement from the events of life. In Zen, as with the Exercises and with Yoga, precisely the very opposite is sought: 'non-heart' connotes 'non-self-centredness'. Formulated positively, it implies the capacity to feel compassion for all beings, that compassion (*Karuna*) which is the highest state sought after in Buddhism, together with wisdom (*prajna*). In the same way, in the practice of Zen and in Buddhism generally, the determination to travel the path (*dai-funshi*) is very important. It appears as the sixth way of the eight proposed by Buddha, correct diligence, of which we are continually reminded by the practitioners of meditation. Four levels of aspirants are distinguished, according to their level of determination: those who have a vague desire to sit down to meditate; those who are after a merely physical or mental improvement; those who desire to achieve illumination but are doing so slowly through the course of many lives; and those who really yearn to achieve the buddhic nature in this life, and who consecrate themselves to it with all their strength.

1.9 OBSTACLES

The Ignatian pathway begins by existentially taking note of what in the biblical tradition is called sin: a conscious positioning within self-centredness. This has direct repercussions on one's relationship with God, with neighbours and with things, obscuring them in the absolutism of our ego. As well as explicit sin, it also seeks to take note of what Saint Ignatius calls *disordered affections*. Up to the moment of making an election, in the centre of the journey, the different exercises are dedicated to deactivating the affections which deprive us of liberty and obscure our lucidity. This also works positively, seeking to draw the affections through contemplation of Christ, the model of the divine-humanity, in his life, passion and resurrection. At the same time it is necessary to be attentive to those temptations which come in a time of desolation, which produce distractions or deviations on the way. Other obstacles which one must learn to identify are one's life wounds which distort our image of God and of our own selves. The healing of these wounds forms a part above all of the objectives of the First Week, although they continue to fester through the whole process, and in each one of the Weeks they are being healed on a more profound level.

The obstacles which impede the way of Yoga (of union) are self-centred desires (*kama*). It is these which cause ignorance (*avidya*) to the point of creating a belief that one exists in separation from the totality. The consciousness of the self-centred I is called *ahamkara*, that which disappears by means of meditation. However, in order for meditation to be possible, it is necessary to practice impartiality, that is, indifference. For this one must add defeat of the disturbances of the mind (*vritti*), which are the unconscious desires that emerge into the consciousness and disturb meditation.

As with Yoga, in Zen the two obstacles are desire and ignorance. This brings us to the Buddhist doctrine of desire, which is the basis of the *Four Noble Truths* pronounced by the Buddha. The first truth is that the human being lives in sorrow; the second, that the cause of this sorrow is the desires. One needs to understand well what kind of desires are being referred to by the

Buddha as the root of suffering. The word he uses is not *kama* (translatable as *eros*), but *trishna*, greed. That is to say, the desire which is fatal is not the movement which makes us feel alive and draws us out of ourselves toward the other, but autocentric greed. It is very similar, therefore, to the disordered affections of Saint Ignatius. This brings us to the third truth; that it is possible to bring an end to suffering by means of indifference or detachment. The fourth truth diffracts into eight paths which Buddha proposes for the practice of indifference: correct vision, correct understanding, correct speech, correct action, the way of correct life, correct diligence, correct attention, and correct concentration. The first two ways are cognitive, so as to orient the process properly; the following three are ethical, so as to achieve a life in conformity with the proposed ideals, and to transform reality; the last three refer more explicitly to the practice of meditation. In Zen they acquire a particular density. In this force for concentration, one of the obstacles which has to be overcome are the *makyo*, visual or auditory hallucinations which emerge during the practice of meditation. When the mind is confronted with emptiness, the subconscious rebels, throwing up images which disperse. The discipline of meditation is to allow these images to appear without being distracted by them.

1.10 Types of Awareness

The Exercises seek to develop two types of cognitive qualities: discernment and internal awareness. Discernment consists in learning to detect the movements of the heart as to whether they lead to life or death, to other-centredness or self-centredness. This makes possible the identification of the will of God, as a kind of sixth sense which allows us to recognise his manifestation. The

Exercises connect up with the whole Christian tradition which dates back to the Desert Fathers, in which we encounter Diadochus of Photice speaking of this gift of discernment as a quality of spiritual awareness.[9] Likewise Saint Paul mentions it (Rom 12:2; 1 Cor 2:6–16). The second type of cognitive quality is that which Ignatius calls 'internal awareness'. This expression appears three times in the course of the Exercises: in the First Week, referring to the profound awareness of the evil of one's own sin (EE 63), that is, of that which separates us from life with God; in the Second Week, referring to 'internal knowledge of the Lord, who became man for me, so that I may love and follow him more' (EE 104), and in the Fourth Week, in the Contemplation for Attaining Love, so as to take 'interior knowledge of so much gift received'. (EE 233) What is distinctive about this awareness is its transforming character. That is to say, it not only informs, but also transforms, to the extent that the various dimensions of the person have been opened up by its influence.

None of this is far from the way of Yoga nor that of Zen.

Discernment is also practised in Hinduism, but here it does not refer to the motions of the good and bad spirit, but to the knowledge which distinguishes between what is permanent and what is impermanent. This discernment (*viveka*) consists in taking care that the individual 'I' is not separated from the Totality, but is immersed in the single Being which is the fount of what exists. The transforming awareness is known in Hinduism by the term *jnana*, which comes from the same root as *gnosis* and *gen*, 'to be born'. It is to do with a consciousness which engenders a new relation to some-

---

[9] 'Ten Chapters on Spiritual Perfection'.

thing of which it is aware. However, one encounters another comparison with the term *anubhava*, which denotes the personal transforming experience which converts the yogi into something which before was only known mentally. The *Upanishads* can only be understood through this experiential awareness.

In Zen, we find the parallels with Ignatian discernment and *viveka hindu* in the notion of 'vigilant attention' (*samyak smriti*), the seventh of the eight practices of the Buddhist way mentioned above. This is to do with living in a state of continuous attention, in which each act is done consciously. This does not produce tension, but quite the opposite. To be present to the present instant means that each moment is experienced in all its fragrance, instead of living devoured by incessant agitation. We can compare this to Ignatian discernment to the extent that it similarly implies an attentive gaze at how we are affected by what we live, so that we adjust our response. The practice of the *Awareness Examen* (EE 24–43), which should be made twice a day, makes the same point. Corresponding to Ignatian 'internal awareness', in Zen there is what is called *prajna*, wisdom, considered one of the most precious fruits. It comes to whoever, through the practice of meditation, has succeeded in unifying contemplation and action. The kind of grasp and intuition of reality which emanates from the *koans* and which results in the silence of *zazen* is translated into the resolution of the paradoxes and contradictions which life presents, always new and unforeseeable.

1.11 ACCOMPANIMENT

The last element of the table is likewise common to the three ways: accompaniment. In the same way that the

Exercises are inconceivable unless there is someone who proposes them and accompanies the discernment. The practice of Yoga and Zen similarly require the guidance of a master.

Initiation into Yoga is inconceivable without the direction of a *guru*. *Gu-ru* means, etymologically, 'someone who dispels the darkness'. The *guru* is the one who helps to determine the postures (*asanas*), the breathing exercises (*pranayamas*), and more particularly, the one who chooses the *mantra* appropriate to each yogi. Insofar as the *mantra* consists of a sound whose careful repetition produces transformations in the mind, in the psyche and in the energetic field of the practitioner, its vibratory effect needs to be adapted to each person. It follows that each one has his particular *mantra* which should not be exchanged, since what is good for one person is not necessarily so for another. But this is not simply about proposing specific practices on the part of the guru, but also the heart of the Hindu experience as occurs in initiation. This is explained in the term *Upanishad*,[10] which means: 'to be seated together with'. This indicates that we are dealing with a doctrine transmitted from master to disciple. Its content cannot be understood outside of this context. The parallels with the little book of the Exercises is remarkable: Ignatius thought of it as a book for the master, to be broken down within the relation between accompanier and accompanied. To read it without practising it does not transform, only distracts, as is the case with the *Upanishads*.

In the practice of *Zen* the relation between master and disciple is likewise essential. 'Zen is a special transmission from heart to heart, on the margin of words and

---

[10] These are writings dateable from the eighth to the fourth centuries before Christ. Although there are 200 different *Upanishads*, the best known number about ten.

letters; aimed directly at the human heart, it brings to view nature itself and converts it into an awakened being', says Bodhidharma, the legendary founder of Zen in China.[11] This contact is particularly present during the *dokusan*, the interview with the master. In the common room, where meditation is practised, those who wish wait in turn to have a meeting with him. The master (*Roshi, Osho*) receives them individually and asks about their difficulties, proposing *koans* which the practitioner has to resolve in the subsequent meditations. In a subsequent interview it will be the master who discerns whether the resolution communicated by the exercitant is only mental, or whether he has grasped it with his body, mind and heart, that is to to say with the whole of his being.

2. DYNAMISMS

Having presented the key elements of each tradition, we now move on to see them within their own respective dynamisms, in order to be able to compare them.

2.1 THE SPIRITUAL EXERCISES AND YOGA

Let us establish the comparison of the Exercises and Yoga on the basis of two classical texts of Hinduism: the *Yoga Sutras* of Yoga Patanjali (between the third century BC and the fifth century AD) and the doctrine of the *Bhagavad Gita* (second century BC).

---

[11] Cited by: Ursula Baatz, *Hugo M. Enomiya-Lassalle. Una vida entre mundos*, Col. Religiones en Diálogo 11, DDB, Bilbao, 2001, p. 22.

2.1.1 The *Yoga Sutras*

The systematization of the *Yoga Sutras* was attributed to Patanjali (the dating is imprecise: between the third century BC and the fifth century AD).[12] These aphorisms do not seem to convey anything new in terms of what was already practised at that time, but they had the merit of presenting with great clarity the essence of a pathway which went back several centuries. The yogic way is set out in eight stages (YS II, 28–29): *Yama, Niyama, Asana, Pranayama, Pratyahara, Dharana, Dhyana* and *Samadhi*. The first five are called external aids to Yoga (*bahiranga sadhana*):

a. *Yama* refers to the five abstentions. These are the same as the five vows of Jainism.
   1. *Ahimsa*: non-violence, inflicting no injury or harm to others or even to one's ownself, it goes as far as nonviolence in thought, word and deed.
   2. *Satya*: truth in word and thought.
   3. *Asteya*: non-covetousness, to the extent that one should not even desire something that is not his own.
   4. *Brahmacharya*: abstain from sexual intercourse; celibacy in the case of unmarried people and monogamy in the case of married people. This even to the extent that one should not possess any sexual thoughts towards any other man or woman except one's own spouse. It is common to associate Brahmacharya with celibacy.
   5. *Aparigraha*: non-possessiveness.

---

[12] There are several editions available in English, including Pantanjali, *Yoga Sutras*, HarperCollins Publishers India, New Delhi.

b. *Niyama* refers to the five observances.
   1. *Shaucha*: cleanliness of body & mind.
   2. *Santosha*: satisfaction; satisfied with what one has.
   3. *Tapas*: austerity and associated observances for bodily discipline & thereby mental control.
   4. *Svadhyaya*: study of the Vedic scriptures to know about God and the soul, which leads to introspection on a greater awakening to the soul and God within.
   5. *Ishvarapranidhana*: surrender to (or worship of) God.

c. *Asana*: Discipline of the body through rules and postures to keep it disease-free and for preserving vital energy. Correct postures are a physical aid to meditation, for they control the limbs and nervous system and prevent them from producing disturbances. The *Hatha Yoga* is the school which has most developed this state, in which many postures are practised, all of them with a specific intention both with respect to muscular elasticity and to the stimulation of the glands and the energy centres. *Ha-* means the solar, masculine, aspect, while *-tha* refers to the lunar, feminine aspect.

d. *Pranayama*: control of breath. Beneficial to health, steadies the body and is highly conducive to the concentration of the mind. *Prana* is not only air, but all the cosmic energy contained in it. Here too there are multiple exercises. *Pranayama* is the most efficient means for developing the *siddhis*, that is to say, the yogic 'powers', such as undertaking long fasts and other corporeal austerities, as well as phenomena such as clairvoyance, etc. One of the temptations for the exercitant of yoga is to be fascinated and trapped by these psychic phenomena.

e. *Pratyahara*: withdrawal of senses from their external objects. This means no sight, no hearing, no speech, in order to be able to have access to a fuller, more truthful way of seeing, hearing and speaking. This is popularly represented by the figure of three monkeys, one of whom covers the eyes, the other the ears, the other the mouth.

These are the external or non-essential steps (*Bahiranga*). The last three levels are called internal aids to Yoga (*antaranga sadhana*), which some currents identify with *Raja Yoga* (Royal Yoga):

f. *Dharana*: concentration of the *citta* (deep mind) upon a physical object, such as a flame of a lamp, the midpoint of the eyebrows, or the image of a deity. This consists in concentrating the attention of the mind on a single object, either externally visualised or imagined interiorly. There are multiple techniques and resources available for this.

g. *Dhyana*: steadfast meditation. Undisturbed flow of thought around the object of meditation. That is to say, a fluid and continuous attention of the mind on a specific aspect of God or of the cosmos or of the self. The act of meditation and the object of meditation remain distinct and separate.

h. *Samadhi*: oneness with the object of meditation. Mircea Elíade uses the word 'enstasis'[13] to distinguish from ecstasis, which would be more specific to the Christian mystical tradition. It refers to a state of absorption in one's own interiority, one where the

---

[13] Cf. *Yoga, Immortality and Freedom* (1956), Princeton Univ. Press, 1973, p. 77.

atman (each one's personal spirit) identifies itself with the *Para-Atman* (the Universal Spirit), being transported beyond ordinary notions of space and time. The result of *samadhi* is the identification of the one meditating with that which is meditated. There is no distinction between the act of meditation and the object of meditation.

Samadhi is of two kinds:

1 *Samadhi conscious samadhi*: when the mind remains concentrated on the object of meditation, therefore the consciousness of the object of meditation persists. Mental modifications arise only in respect of this object of meditation.

2 *Asamprajnata Samadhi supraconscious*: when the mind and the object of meditation are fused together. The consciousness of the object of meditation is transcended.[14] All mental modifications are checked, although latent impressions may continue. Combined simultaneous practice of *Dharana*, *Dhyana* & *Samadhi* is referred to as *Samyama*.

The sequence of these eight steps contains parallels with the Ignatian exercises, as well as differences. The first two (renunciations – *yamas* – and observances – *niyamas*) refer to the basic ethical attitudes before beginning the way, which we may relate to the Annotations of the Exercises and with the *Principles and Foundation*, as well as to many aspects of the First Week. More particularly the similarity between the five renunciations (*yamas*) and the last six precepts of the Hebrew decalogue, or with the seven deadly sins which are proposed for meditation in the first mode of prayers

---

[14] In some sense, this distinction corresponds to the difference between a personal God or one with attributes (*Saguna Brahman*), and an impersonal or apophatic God (*Brahman Nirguna*).

in the Exercises. (EE 244-245) It is important to take into account that both for Yoga and the Exercises, the indispensable requirements for practice are not merely to do with understanding, but they involve the integral commitment of the person.

The next two (bodily postures – *asanas* – and respiratory exercises – *pranayama*) correspond to some extent to the Notes and Annotations of the Exercises. On the other hand, here the ways diverge, since for Ignatius, corporeal disposition is merely preparatory, while in Yoga it is the vehicle of meditation, to the point of not needing scriptural passages. That is to say, the body and the breathing, as with Zen, are converted into supports for meditation.

The fifth stage, the withdrawl of the senses (*pratyahara*), can be aligned with the general withdrawal required by the Exercises, according to Annotation 20, but also by the penitential character of the First Week, where sight and the senses in general are contained. (EE 79-85) From the point of view of content, this fifth stage is also related generally to the First Week, insofar as withdrawal of the senses is very close to being conscious of disordered affections and reordering them, as is attempted in the first Ignatian stage.

The three final stages (concentration, meditation, and absorption) have on the one hand a certain correspondence to the Ignatian progression (meditation-consideration-contemplation). In both ways there is an advance in the meditative capacity, such that ever greater depths are reached, where that which is contemplated and the one who contemplates are becoming one. On the other hand, the methods offered in Yoga to achieve concentration and the vehicles for meditation are greatly varied, which we next find at the climax of the Exercises. Both ways differ enormously from Zen which is much more restrained.

From the point of view of the difference and the

specificity of each way, the ascent of Yoga – which is at the same time a descent into the cave of the heart, into the inner sanctuary (*Garbha Griha*) – seeks to achieve the kind absorption (*samadhi*) we have already mentioned. The ideal of Yoga is to prolong this state for as long as possible, which in advanced yogis can last uninterrupted for several days. This is not, directly, what the Exercises seek to achieve. Certainly it is hoped that they can provide unitive moments in which 'our Lord himself communicates Himself to the devout soul, that he inflame it with his love and praise' (EE 15), causing all mediation between Creator and creature to disappear ('immediate', EE 15,6) and 'entering, leaving and acting upon the soul to draw it wholly to his love'. (EE 330) In sum, the end of the Exercises is to find the will of God for each life. That will can manifest itself in the state of *samadhi*, that is, for the First Time of Election, in which 'Our Lord God, so moves and attracts the will that a devout soul without hesitation, or the possibility of hesitation, follows what has been manifested to it.' (EE 175) But the summit is not this state of absorption, but the *Contemplation for Attaining Love*, which is more similar to the *satori* of Zen which, as we shall see, ends with the return to the marketplace.

What I wish to say is that the specificity of Yoga is to align some spiritual practices (*sadhana*) to achieve silencing, which produces a profound internal unification and pacification. The Exercises, in not going directly in search of this silence but of the election, do not obtain such quietude nor perhaps such depth in their own interiority, because they are in process of discerning on decisions which affect the exterior life. Their objective is not so much permanency in interiority as a training in turning to the exterior, without losing it. This 'return' is not explicitly considered in the eight classical stages of Yoga.

2.1.2. The Three *Yogas* of the Bhagavad Gita

A deep engagement with Yoga makes clear that it consists not solely in the practice of specified exercises (*sadhana*), but in something much more radical: it is one of the Hindu names to refer to access to full realisation. Classically, three ways are identified: the way or yoga of action (*Karma*), the way or yoga of devotion (*Bhakti*) and the way or yoga of knowledge (*jnana*). These three ways are synthesised in the *Bhagavad Gita* (BG), '*The Song of the Lord*,' a work written around the third century BC, which makes a synthesis of the different currents of the epoch. Together with the *Upanishads*, it is considered an integral part of the *Vedanta*, 'Final of the Vedas', which elevates it to the category of revelation (*sruti*).[15] It was incorporated into the *Mahabharata*, an epic poem seven times longer than the *Iliad*, although evidently it does not belong to the genre of the epic-mythic, but to the mystical. Its parallelisms with the Gospels are such that the first western studies date them to the second or third centuries of our era, convinced that they contained Christian influences. On the other hand, the majority of contemporary experts are agreed in dating them to the third century before Christ.

The *Karma Yoga* is treated in chapters 3, 4 and 5; the *Bhakti Yoga*, in chapters 9, 11, 12 and 15; and the *Jnana Yoga,* in chapters 2, 4, 6, 7 and 13. This assignation is a simplification which risks betraying the complexity of the text. At times it has been presented with even greater simplification: the Yoga of action has

---

[15] *Sruti* means 'audition', 'that which has been heard' by the inspired clairvoyants (*rishi*). It refers to a manifestation, epiphany, rumour, echo, music, sonority of the Ultimate Reality.

been identified with the first seven chapters; the Yoga of knowledge with chapters 7–13 and the Yoga of love with the remainder, as if the *Bhagavad Gita* is an ascending progression from action to love passing through knowledge. Although such a distribution is pedagogical and suggestive, it does not respect the complexity of the text, where the character of the three ways is not hierarchical but circular. It is this quality which brings a surprising similarity to the Exercises.

a. The Yoga Karma or the Yoga of Action

The text begins by presenting prince Arjuna, of the dynasty of Bharata, facing his army before doing battle against his parents because they have illegitimately usurped the throne. Arjuna has doubts about attacking them and wants to avoid the conflict. Krishna (godhead) shows himself to him in the form of the archer who drives his chariot, telling him that he cannot shirk his responsibility, but that he must act without hatred, with equanimity, moved by a sense of justice, liberated from the incumbrances of the 'I'. This is presented as the first way, or yoga: action, which consists in doing things in a decentred way, in the service of the cosmic order. From the beginning it is said with clarity that the Supreme Being is not passive but active:

One does not attain freedom from the bondage of Karma by merely abstaining from work. No one attains perfection by merely giving up work. (3,4)

O Arjuna, there is nothing in the three worlds (earth, heaven, and the upper regions) that should be done by Me, nor is there anything unobtained that I should obtain, yet I engage in action. Because, if I do not engage in action relentlessly, O Arjuna, people would follow My path in every way. (3,22-23)

This is not any action whatsoever, but one which takes place without any turning upon oneself. It is a free, disinterested, gratuitous action:

> The one who rejoices in the Self only, who is satisfied with the Self, who is content in the Self alone, for such a self-realised person there is no duty. Such a person has no interest, whatsoever, in what is done or what is not done. A self-realised person does not depend on anybody for anything. (3,17-18)
>
> Therefore, always perform your duty efficiently and without attachment to the results, because by doing work without attachment one attains the Supreme. (3,19)

Repeated verses insist on saying that the essence of the action of the realised person is to act without seeking egocentric interests:

> As the ignorant work, O Arjuna, with attachment to the fruits of work, so the wise should work without attachment, for the welfare of the society. (3,25)
>
> Dedicating all works to Me in a spiritual frame of mind, free from desire, attachment, and mental grief, do your duty. (3,30)
>
> Works do not bind Me, because I have no desire for the fruits of work. The one who understands this truth is also not bound by Karma. (4,14)

A person whose works are free from selfish desires and motives, and whose whole Karma is burned up in the fire of Self-knowledge, is called a sage by the wise. (4,19)

Relating this to the Exercises, we are fully in the atmosphere of the *Principle and Foundation*, where we are presented with human existence radically decentred from itself, in praise, reverence and service of God. (EE 23) From this begins the work of disaffection of the First Week and the search for the will of God for one's own life, so as to choose not according to criteria centred on the ego, but to act according to the categories of the Kingdom. The Ignatian maxim that 'each one should keep in mind that in all that concerns the spiritual life his progress will be in proportion to his surrender of self-love and of his own will and interests' (EE 189) has the same resonance as the *Bhagavad Gita*. In both ways the same thing is at stake: to overcome the narrow perspective of the ego and open up to a greater reality where action and commitment are necessary for the transformation of the whole.

b. Bhakti Yoga or the Yoga of Devotion

Some Indian theologians have discussed at what point the concept of *bhakti* corresponds exactly with Christian love.[16] They judge that the more adequate Sanskrit term would be *prema*, which has a more affective and relational character than *bhakti*, which has a more devotional and restrictive character. Nevertheless, we maintain the adequacy of the term *bhakti* since it refers to the energy

---

[16] Cf. George M. Soares-Prabhu, *The Dharma of Jesus*, edited by Francis Xavier D'Sa. Maryknoll, NY, Orbis Books, 2003.

of the heart, just as *jnana* corresponds to the energy of the mind. On the other hand, the root *bhak-*, means 'share'. One could say that Christianity is a religion which is fundamentally *bhaktic*, since it translates completely into the handing over of the person into Christ, in response to his handing himself over to us. For this reason, the following versicles of the *Bhagavad Gita* are extremely relevant:

> The Supreme Lord said: Those ever steadfast devotees who worship with supreme faith by fixing their mind on Me as their personal God, I consider them to be the best yogis. (12,2) (See also 6,47)

> To those who worship Me as the personal God, renouncing all actions to Me; setting Me as their supreme goal, and meditating on Me with single minded devotion; I swiftly become their saviour, from the world that is the ocean of death and transmigration, whose thoughts are set on Me, O Arjuna. (12,6–7)

> Therefore, focus your mind on Me alone and let your intellect dwell upon Me through meditation and contemplation. Thereafter you shall certainly come to Me. (12,8)

> One who does not hate any creature, who is friendly and compassionate, free from the notion of 'I' and 'my', even-minded in pain and pleasure, forgiving; and the yogi who is ever content, who has subdued the mind, whose resolve is firm, whose mind and intellect are engaged in dwelling upon Me; such a devotee is dear to Me. (12,13–14)

The Ignatian Execises fully stimulate this affective-devotional way to Jesus, through contemplation of the Gospels. Attraction to his person is one of the keys to the transformation which is activated in the exercitant, to the point of arriving at full identification with him.

c. *The Jnana Yoga or the Yoga of Knowledge*

The third way of realisation is through knowledge. This does not mean a mental knowledge, but integral and experiential, the result of having centred the entirety of one's attention on the Supreme Being, by means of the dicipline of meditation:

> Supreme bliss comes to a Self-realised yogi whose mind is quiet, whose desires are under control, and who is free from sin. (6,27)

> Such a sinless yogi, who constantly engages the mind with the Self, easily enjoys the infinite bliss of contact with Brahman. (6,28)

> Because of perceiving the same Self abiding in all beings and all beings abiding in the same Self; a yogi, who is in union with the Self, sees every being with an equal eye. (6,29) (See also 4,35)

> Those who see Me in everything and see everything in Me, are not separated from Me and I am not separated from them. (6,30)

> I am the origin or seed of all beings, O Arjuna. There is nothing, animate or inanimate, that can exist without Me. (10,39) (See also 7,10 and 9,18)

> There is no end of My divine manifestations, O Arjuna. This is only a brief description by Me of the extent of My divine manifestations. (10,40)
>
> Whatever is endowed with glory, brilliance, and power; know that to be a manifestation of a fraction of My splendour. (10,41)
>
> What is the need for this detailed knowledge, O Arjuna? I continually support the entire universe by a small fraction of My energy. (10,42)

The perception of the divine presence in everything leads to a veneration and respect for all the manifestations of reality, so that the realised person is capable of seeing God – the Absolute – in all things:

> An enlightened person looks at a learned and humble Brahmana, an outcast, even a cow, an elephant, or a dog with an equal eye. (5,18)

We are fully in the atmosphere of the 'Contemplation for Attaining Love' in the Ignatian Exercises, where one arrives at a level of perception similar to contemplating how God has impregnated the whole of reality:

> See how God inhabits creatures: in the elements, giving them being, in the plants vegetable life, in the animals sensation, and in human beings understanding. (EE 235)
>
> Consider how he works and labours for me in created things ... (EE 236)
>
> Consider how all goods and gifts descend from above. (EE 237)

The distinctive characteristic of the way of knowledge is the entry into the divine sphere through meditation on the ultimate reality. We are at the heart of the Vedanta: 'Know a *Brahman* and you will convert yourself into a *Brahman*,' says one *Upanishad*.[17] This affirmation is the basis of the doctrine of *advaita*, the non-duality of God and creature which the yogi who practises the path of knowledge seeks to perceive. To some extent, this is the same goal of the Ignatian Exercises which ultimately attains identification with Christ, in a way that he ceases to be the object of contemplation so as to become the *place* from which everything is contemplated. With the offering of 'Take, Lord, receive' the exercitant is almost repeating the words of Christ in the Eucharist so as to open up to reality in all its radiance. The internal knowledge of Christ which has been petitioned throughout the Second Week (EE 104) has been converted at the end of the Exercises into the complete reality of the exercitant who can now say with Saint Paul: 'It is no longer I that live, but Christ who lives in me.' (Gal 2:20)

What is important in the doctrine of the *Bhagavad Gita* is its constant affirmation that through the three one can come to the realization of the human being, which consists in the discovery that we exist inseparably from the Absolute Being. The novelty of the *Bhagavad Gita* – and this is what makes it such a popular work in Hinduism – is in considering the complementarity of the three ways for achieving such fulfilment. Its integrative capacity is reflected in these verses:

> If you are unable to meditate or focus your mind steadily on Me, then seek to reach Me, O Arjuna, by practice of any other spiritual discipline (*sadhana*) of your choice. (12,9)

[17] *Mundaka Up.* 3,29.

If you are unable even to do any *sadhana*, then be intent on performing your duty for Me. You shall attain perfection just by working for Me as an instrument, just to serve and please Me, without selfish motives. (12,10) (See also 9, 27; 18,46)

If you are unable to work for Me then just surrender unto My will with subdued mind, and renounce the attachment to, and the anxiety for, the fruits of all work by learning to accept all results, as God-given, with equanimity. (12,11)

In the same way, we may say that these three ways are present in the Ignatian Exercises. They appear to be mentioned explicitly in the petition of the Second Week, which we may consider to be a condensation of this entire pathway:

To pray for internal knowledge of Our Lord Jesus Christ, so that we may better love and serve him. (EE 104)

Knowledge sustains love, and love, discipleship. Union with Christ is an endless movement which comes to be realised through this inseparable interrelation between three factors: the action which is realised as a result of discernment – the cognitive way – of the will of God, is converted into the way of union, not only personal but also cosmic. The Ignatian mystagogy consists, as in the *Bhagavad Gita*, in unifying these three dimensions into one, in an integration each time more profound and harmonious, between behaviour, graced knowledge and self-offering.

Now we move to see what happens in Zen.

2.2 THE SPIRITUAL EXERCISES AND ZEN

I will compare the Ignatian way with Zen by means of the ten pictures of the bull made by Kuo-an, a Chinese monk of the twelfth century. The search for and capture of the bull by a peasant serves as a metaphor to show the steps through which the practitioner of Zen must pass, so as to attain illumination. Each picture includes three parts: a strophe of a poem of Kuo-an followed by the commentary which he introduces himself[18] and some clarifications from me.

---

[18] According to the version adapted by Nyogen Senzaki and Paul Reps in the first edition of their translation.

1. The Search for the Bull.
2. Discovering the Footprints.
3. Perceiving the Bull.
4. Catching the Bull.
5. Taming the Bull.

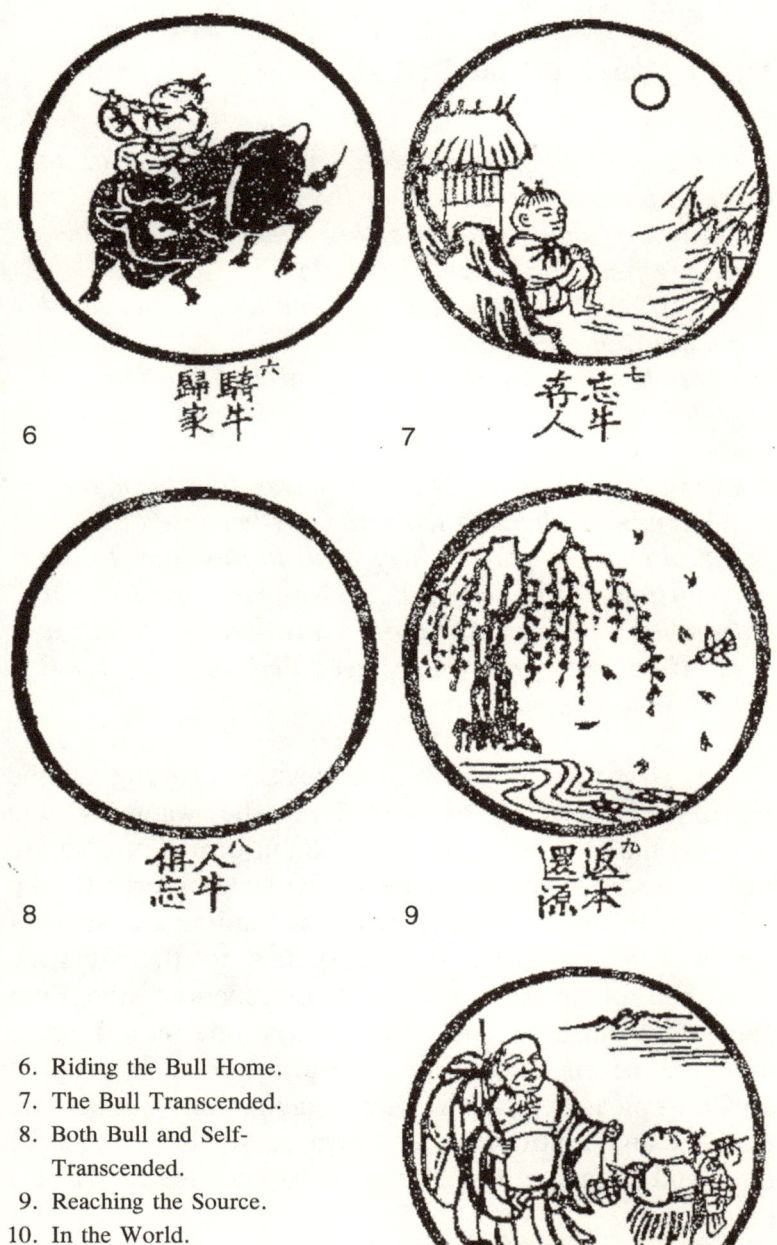

6. Riding the Bull Home.
7. The Bull Transcended.
8. Both Bull and Self-Transcended.
9. Reaching the Source.
10. In the World.

1. The Search for the Bull

In the pasture of this world, I endlessly push aside the tall grasses in search of the bull.
Following unnamed rivers, lost upon the interpenetrating paths of distant mountains,
My strength failing and my vitality exhausted, I cannot find the bull.
I only hear the locusts chirring through the forest at night.

Comment in prose: *The bull never has been lost. What need is there to search? Only because of separation from my true nature, I fail to find him. In the confusion of the senses I lose even his tracks. Far from home, I see many crossroads, but which way is the right one I know not. Greed and fear, good and bad, entangle me.*

In this first picture we see the peasant entering on the journey. Everything disturbs him: the waterfall, the parrots, the butterflies. A way without direction. We are in a phase prior to commitment, the state before starting off on whichever spiritual way that implies a change of life and of attitudes. It corresponds to the situation described in the first rule of discernment of the First Week: 'In those persons who go from one mortal sin to another, the enemy is ordinarily accustomed to propose apparent pleasures, filling their imagination with sensual delights and gratifications, the more so as to preserve them and augment them in their vices and sins'. (EE 314)

2. Discovering the Footprints

Along the riverbank under the trees, I discover footprints!
Even under the fragrant grass I see his prints.
Deep in remote mountains they are found.
These traces no more can be hidden than one's nose, looking heavenward.

Comment in prose: *Understanding the teaching, I see the footprints of the bull. Then I learn that, just as many utensils are made from one metal, so too are myriad entities made of the fabric of self. Unless I discriminate, how will I perceive the true from the untrue? Not yet having entered the gate, nevertheless I have discerned the path.*

The first traces of the bull have motivated the peasant, who begins to search with determination. We are before the forcefulness of the Principle and Foundation, and before the renunciations and adhesions of Yoga.

3. Perceiving the Bull

I hear the song of the nightingale.
The sun is warm, the wind is mild, willows are green along the shore,
Here no bull can hide!
What artist can draw that massive head, those majestic horns?

Comment in prose: *When one hears the voice, one can sense its source. As soon as the six senses merge, the gate is entered. Wherever one enters one sees the head of the bull! This unity is like salt in water, like color in dyestuff. The slightest thing is not apart from self.*

For the first time the peasant makes out the bull at the back. We are given here the first indications of illumination. We may relate this third state with the *Annotations and Additions* of the Exercises, insofar as they dispose a person for meditation. In Yoga, we encounter this in the practice of postures (*asanas*) and the respiratory exercises (*pranayama*).

4. Catching the Bull

I seize him with a terrific struggle.
His great will and power are inexhaustible.
He charges to the high plateau far above the cloud-mists,
Or in an impenetrable ravine he stands.

Comment in prose: *He dwelt in the forest a long time, but I caught him today! Infatuation for scenery interferes with his direction. Longing for sweeter grass, he wanders away. His mind still is stubborn and unbridled. If I wish him to submit, I must raise my whip.*

In order to capture the bull one must struggle with him. In the practice of Zen, this phase corresponds to the difficulties one has when dealing with distractions, discomforts and pains in the seating posture, drowsiness, dreams, the emergence of one's shadows during the meditation ... This phase clearly correlates with the struggles of the First Week and the invitation to penance (EE 82–89), and, in Yoga, with the power to recover and master the senses.

5. Taming the Bull

The whip and rope are necessary,
Else he might stray off down some dusty road.
Being well trained, he becomes naturally gentle.
Then, unfettered, he obeys his master.

Comment in prose: *When one thought arises, another thought follows. When the first thought springs from enlightenment, all subsequent thoughts are true. Through delusion, one makes everything untrue. Delusion is not caused by objectivity; it is the result of subjectivity. Hold the nose-ring tight and do not allow even a doubt.*

In this fifth picture the peasant succeeds in becoming the bull. It is the most stable phase in the practice of meditation. We may relate it to the Ignatian meditation on the Eternal King (EE 91–98), at the start of the Second Week, in which the values of Jesus begin to be internalised. It corresponds to the fifth stage of Yoga, concentration.

6. Riding the Bull Home

Mounting the bull, slowly I return homeward.
The voice of my flute intones through the evening.
Measuring with hand-beats the pulsating harmony,
I direct the endless rhythm.
Whoever hears this melody will join me.

Comment in prose: *This struggle is over; gain and loss are assimilated. I sing the song of the village woodsman, and play the tunes of the children.*

Astride the bull, I observe the clouds above. Onward I go, no matter who may wish to call me back.

In such a way the bull has become familiarised with the peasant, so that he can be utilised as a mount to return home, avoiding the tiredness of the walker. Here, the practitioner of Zen is acquiring a meditation each time more fluid. It can be compared to the contemplations of the Second Week of the Exercises, where kind hours pass before the passages of the gospel, and where something of the interior knowledge of Jesus which we have mentioned is attained. (EE 104)

7. The Bull Transcended

Astride the bull, I reach home.
I am serene. The bull too can rest.
The dawn has come. In blissful repose,
Within my thatched dwelling I have abandoned the whip and rope.

Comment in prose: *All is one law, not two. We only make the bull a temporary subject. It is like the relation of rabbit and trap, of fish and net. It is like gold and dross, or the moon emerging from a cloud. One path of clear light travels on throughout endless time.*

On his return home, the peasant relaxes serenely, having placed the bull in the stable. Everything is in order. During meditation, states of great peace and harmony are achieved. To some extent we can compare this with the satisfaction produced in the Exercises by the accomplishment of the process of election at the end of the Second Week, having successfully discerned what one is looking for or having made the necessary reform of life. We can also compare this with the Application of the Senses (EE 121–126), an exercise which is proposed for the final day, in which one enters without pressure as if by contagion and distillation of what has been contemplated during the day. The last two pictures can be related to the seventh step of yoga, *dhyana*, in which the yogi enters into a fluid meditation.

8. Both Bull and Self Transcended

Whip, rope, person, and bull, all merge in
  No-Thing.
This heaven is so vast no message can stain it.
How may a snowflake exist in a raging fire?
Here are the footprints of the patriarchs.

Comment in prose: *Mediocrity is gone. Mind is clear of limitation. I seek no state of enlightenment. Neither do I remain where no enlightenment exists. Since I linger in neither condition, eyes cannot see me. If hundreds of birds strew my path with flowers, such praise would be meaningless.*

Here we come to the most important picture of the sequence: a white circle, without any image, which can be interpreted in two ways. In the first place, as the disappearance of the known world of forms, in which the meditator is confronted with the radical loss of the ego. In the Rinzai School the expression Great Death is used, preceded by the Great Doubt. This corresponds to the Passion of the Ignatian Exercises where one has to consider 'how the divinity hides itself'. (EE 196)

But this white circle, without any form or containing all forms, can also be interpreted as the plenitude of the experince of *satori*, complete illumination, in which every-form and non-form are transcended. Dogen (13th century), founder of the Soto School, describes enlightenment in this way:

> The achievement of enlightenment is like the reflection of the moon in the water.
> Neither is the moon moistened nor is the surface of the water disturbed.
> Great is the moon, and full is the radius of its rays of light, but everything fits into a drop of water.
> All the moon and all the heavens are reflected in every dewdrop.
> To not be an obstacle to the enlightenment is to let go of oneself,
> To be no more than a reflection, in the same way as the dewdrop does not impede the reflection of that sky and moon.[19]

This second interpretation would correspond to the *samadhi* of Yoga and to the consolations 'without previous cause' of the Exercises (330), as well as with the Ignatian contemplations of the Fourth Week, in which the Resurrection of Christ transcends every form until the episode of the Ascension. (EE 312)

With this picture the series was completed as was known in the twelfth century. As in the antecendent stages of Yoga until reaching *samadhi*, it culminated in a phase very different from the ordinary state of consciousness. But Kuo-an, a Chinese monk, added two more scenes which were incorporated from then on, and which are suprisingly 'Ignatian'.

---

[19] Cited by: Juan Masiá Clavel, *Budistas y cristianos. Más allá del diálogo*, Cuadernos Fe y Secularidad 39, Sal Terrae, Santander, 1997, p. 29.

9. Reaching the Source: reappearance of shapes and nature as they are

Too many steps have been taken returning to the root and the source.
Better to have been blind and deaf from the beginning!
Dwelling in one's true abode, unconcerned with or without.
The river flows tranquilly on and the flowers are red.

Comment in prose: *From the beginning, truth is clear. Poised in silence, I observe the forms of integration and disintegration. One who is not attached to 'form' need not be 'reformed'. The water is emerald, the mountain is indigo, and I see that which is creating and that which is destroying.*

In the ninth circle we see the return of cascades, parrots, butterflies ... the difference with respect to the first picture is that the diverse elements of nature are not an object of distraction, as at the beginning of the pathway, but an occasion of contemplation. In Zen it is said that before enlightment, the flowers are flowers, the trees are trees and the mountains are mountains; during enlightenment, the flowers cease to be flowers, the trees cease to be trees, and the mountains cease to be mountains; and after enlightenment the flowers return to being flowers, the trees return to being trees, and the mountains return to being mountains. Reality continues the same but is perceived in a different way: no longer self-centredly, though things continuue to manifest their own radiance. All this can be put in clear parallel with the Contemplation for Attaining Love (EE 230-237), where the elements of creation are no longer obstacles to approaching God, but the divine means for coming to Him and through which he approaches us. As is said explicitly in the introduction to the Contemplation:

> Love consists in a mutual sharing of goods, for example the lover gives and shares with the beloved what he possesses, or something of that which he has or is able to give, and vice versa, the beloved shares with the lover; such that if one has knowledge, he shares it with the one who does not possess it; likewise with honours, riches and so on. (EE 231)

If in the course of the Exercises it has been necessary to renounce all this, seeking insults, poverty, madness (EE 98, 147; 167), now one may receive all manner of gifts, because he or she has been liberated from the deformity of self-centred affections, and now all this has been referred to the other, and to the cause of the Kingdom.

10. Return to the market place

Barefooted and naked of breast, I mingle with the people of the world.
My clothes are ragged and dust-laden, and I am ever blissful.
I use no magic to extend my life;
Now, before me, the dead trees become alive.

Comment in prose: *Inside my gate, a thousand sages do not know me. The beauty of my garden is invisible. Why should one search for the footprints of the patriarchs? I go to the market place with my wine bottle and return home with my staff. I visit the wine shop and the market, and everyone I look upon becomes enlightened.*

Surprisingly, the last of the pictures culiminates in a market. In principle, a scene which is hardly appropriate for contemplation. Precisely here is how one verifies the authenticity of the experience of illumination: in its capacity for being maintained in the noise, in the disturbance, in the chaos, and in transmitting itself to others. For this reason, in the final picture the peasant has been transformed into a sage. In our tradition this corresponds to the return to Galilee (Mk 16:7), the end of the gospels and of the Exercises also, the encounter with the risen Christ in everyday life. In this sense, the return to normal life is not the Fifth Week, but the prolongation and extention of the Fourth, insofar as it deals with the recognition of the Risen Lord through the traces of his resurrection. (EE 223)

It must be stressed that this final picture is not far from Buddhism, but reflects its most esteemed figure: the *bodhisattva*, 'he who has realised full enlightenment', renounces entry into *Nirvana* until the last of beings has entered also. In Hinduism this corresponds to the *jivan-mukta*, 'the living person liberated', who transmits through his sole presence the effects of his transfiguration.

We here present the stages we have described in a synoptic table, so that we can compare at a glance the three pathways. Now we are in a slightly better position to take up again the diverse elements and propose a further comparative balance.

YOGA	SPIRITUAL EXERCISES	ZEN
—	Before starting the Sp Ex	1. In distracted search of the bull
yamas (abstentions) *niyamas* (observances)	Annotations and Additions Principle and Foundation First method of prayer	2. Discovery of the footprints
âsanas (postures) *pranayama* (breathing)	Annotations and Additions Principle and Foundation	3. Perceiving the bull
pratyahara (withdrawal of the senses)	20th Annotation Meditations on First Week	4. Catching the bull
pratyahara (withdrawal of the senses) *dharana* (concentration)	Meditations on First Week	5. Taming the bull
dhyana (meditation)	Contemplations on 2nd Week	6. Riding the bull
dharana (concentration)	Resolution about the election	7. The bull transcended
dhyana (meditation)	Contemplations on 3rd week	8. Both bull and self transcended 8.1. Depth Death
Samadhi (absorption)	Contemplations on 4th week Election by first mode Consolation without precedent cause (330)	8. Both bull and self transcended 8.2. *Satori*
Samadhi	Contemplation to obtain love	9. In communion with nature
Jivanmukta (living liberated)	Contemplation to obtain love and return to ordinary life	10. Return to the marketplace

2.3 Development of Some Points

Having familiarised ourselves with the three pathways, we are in a position to reconsider certain aspects which have emerged only fragmentarily. Now we can tackle their divergent and convergent points with greater perspective and make them more precise. I emphasise that the Ignatian Exercises are within the tradition of the positive way: with respect to God, insofar as it recognises attributes which are accessible for the intellect and the affections; and for its anthropological conception, putting in play the various human capacities as vehicles by which to attain the region of the divine. At the extreme opposite is Zen, which is perhaps the most radical expression of the *via negativa* which belongs to Buddhism as a religion, which is essentially apophatic. Its silence over the Ultimate Reality as well as the void of the psychic and mental meditations which we encounter in Zen is one of its highest expressions. Between both ways, we find the intermediate way of Yoga and Hinduism as a religion. From here spring the differences which they undoubtedly contain.

a. Presence and absence of images and discursive thought

The first initially divergent element is a consequence of the difference between the *via positiva* and the *via negativa*: the discursiveness and the imaginative actuation of the Exercises over against the absence of images and of mental activity in the later phases of Yoga, and even more radically in Zen. The Ignatian pedagogy uses affective imaginative and mental activity in a way that 'anoints' them for the gospel. In Yoga and in Zen, on the other hand, the option is for the opposite way: to eliminate, from the beginning, all psychic and discursive activity, because they are considered products of the ego, and therefore traps. On the other hand, the doctrinal base of the Exercises is dual: life-death; poverty-riches; honour-humiliation; health-sickness; good spirit-bad spirit; I-Thou ... This statement which, as Westerners, seems obvious to us, even inevitable, is precisely what one seeks to transcend with the non-dual perception *advaita*, where the separation between Creator and creature, between subject and object, between human being and the world, disappears. As the reason functions under the principle of non-contradiction and is constitutively binary, both Yoga and Zen prescind from it. In order to achieve this, they resort to corporal experience, fundamentally through respiration, which is pre-mental and trans-mental. Corporeal consciousness happens in the present, diluting the notion of time, which is sequential; the attention to the continuous flow of air in the body replaces mental elaboration. One only has consciousness of the present. In the Exercises, on the other hand, the sequence of past (memory), present (call), and future (in view of the election) is very much taken into account, as we shall see in what follows.

b. On the historical dimension, the election and the action which lead to commitment

The essence of the Ignatian way is the discernment of a decision. This configures and structures an entire spirituality and a way of conceiving the experience of God and a way of being in the world. The Exercises trace the pathway of a search, freeing the disordered affections so as to achieve the liberty which will permit a free and lucid action. This intention is not made explicit either in

Yoga or in Zen. On the other hand, if the practice is correct, this is also accomplished, as the transformation which is produced leads in each case to the taking of appropriate decisions, insofar as the ego has been dissolved. In the final analysis, the definitive election of the Exercises is to allow oneself to be possessed by God, which is where the other two pathways lead.

From the point of view of Yoga and Zen, the Exercises run the danger of remaining in small steps, instead of undertaking the flight of the eagle, which allows one to see a landscape in perspective, rather than having no idea of it. From the point of view of the Exercises, the practice of Yoga and of Zen lack credibility if they do not lead to decisions which commit the meditator to his environment.

c. Effort and grace

Another theme which we have not yet addressed is the articulation between gift and task, between grace and effort. According to what is understood in the practices of Yoga and Zen, it seems that they depend exclusively on the determination and will of their practitioners; among other things because, especially in Zen, there is no 'Thou' to whom one can refer. On this complex question, we may make the following observations:

A difficult paradox must be maintained in the three ways: the 'I' cannot be delegated, since it is this 'I' which one must learn to hand over. Grace does not supplant effort, but this strength is not a strength of the ego, which is immune to grace, but is precisely that which permits the abandonment of the ego so that grace may enter.

The articulation of grace-effort in the Exercises is not simple. With good reason they have frequently been accused of Pelagianism. Even if all the meditations begin with two prayers of petition for the gift which one desires to receive (EE 46 and 48), nevertheless, they also speak of 'always being intent on seeking what I desire.' (EE 76) Without this determination of one's own desire there is no anthropological basis for taking this pathway. 'There is no subject' (EE 18,8), according to the expression of St Ignatius.

We have seen that Hinduism recognises the *bhaktic* dimension, where confidence and handing over to God are what permit achievement of the final goal: 'All those who seek their refuge in Me, no matter how weak or sinful they may be, will for certain attain the Supreme Way'. (BG 9,32)[20] The name *Shiva* itself means: 'he who bestows grace'. Devotional Yoga, therefore, is fully rooted in the knowledge that access to the divine is gift. The question is more problematic in the strict ambit of the way of knowledge (*Jnana Marga*), where the concept of grace cannot be understood relationally, but has to be described in another way: in terms of receptivity, of gratuity, and not of personal achievement or self-reference. This is precisely what has to be defeated: the voluntarism of the ego. This is achieved by means of experiential knowledge (*anubhava*) of onself as part of a Whole greater than oneself. Grace, is therefore contained in the same knowledge: transformative and dissolving of the ego.

Undoubtedly, Zen has a more severe aspect, probably due to its connection over a long period of time with the discipline of the samurai, warrior monks. Nevertheless there is also within it a space for gratitude, a grace which is related with the force of *hara*, situated in the centre of the being, opposed to the control of the ego. This is illustrated in a story told by a German scholar

---

[20] See also: BG 9, 18.22. 26. 27.30.34; 18,65.68.

who spent years in a Buddhist monastery. What cost him most was the exercise of archery because he strained to launch the arrow with the tension of the arms and of the will, while the master indicated to him that the arrow had to be shot only with the energy of *hara*. After years of strained frustrations, one day, without knowing how, the arrow landed placidly in the centre of the bullseye. The master, surprised, approached the disciple and bowed before him. The Westerner very proudly exclaimed: 'Thank you!' To which the master replied: Are you still so obtuse as to believe that I am bowing to you? It is to the Force which came out of you that I am bowing'.[21]

d. Extinction of the ego and decentring as a way of transformation

To achieve the Ultimate Reality the three ways consider, with equal radicality, that an abandonment and extinction of the ego is required. This goal is expressed according to the language of each tradition. The three ways converge on the understanding that one only comes to plenitude by means of some form or other of death. So, in the Exercises we find this sentence: 'For every one must keep in mind that in all that concerns the spiritual life his progress will be in proportion to his surrender of self-love and his own will and interests.' (EE 189) This sentence is preceded by the Three Degrees of Humility (EE 165–167), which culminate in poverty by way of an absence of things; in dishonour by way of an absence of social and affective relations, which leads to the loss of social image; and madness, through the absence of knowledge. We encounter these evacuations in the offering of the five 'alls' at the end of the Exercises: 'Take,

---

[21] Eugen Herrigel, *Zen in the Art of Archery*, Penguin, New York 1988, ch. 7.

Lord, and receive, *all* my liberty, memory, understanding, and my entire will, *all* I have and possess (...); *all* is yours, dispose of *all* according to your will; give me only your love and your grace and this is enough for me'. (EE 234) These five 'alls' correspond, in turn, to the 'nothings' of St John of the Cross, inviting to a more complete stripping, so as to be able to gain access to the climax of meeting 'the beloved in the Lover transformed'. In handing over everything, one enters in the nothing (the Buddhist *sunyata*), on the threshold of achieving the real Whole. In Yoga one must transcend *ahamkara*, the consciousness of the individual 'I'; while in Zen one must pass through *anahatta,* 'the negation of the "I"', to arrive at the grand Death, and only thus achieve enlightenment. In Buddhist terms, Jesus did not have an 'I' as such (*atta*), but the I of God, which is constitutively *kenotic*. In the words of Aloysius Pieris: 'Jesus is the ec-centric act of God to the search for the centre of God outside the divine circle, in the human other'.[22] And again: 'To recognise that one's 'I' lacks real existence except in relation to the Other is the wisdom (*prajna*) which comes to us from the cross, *gnosis* welling up from *ágape*'.[23]

e. Presence and absence of a divine 'Thou'

From the doctrinal and structural point of view, one nuclear question needs to be resolved: that which distinguishes the Exercises is their christocentrism. Their proposal is inconceivable without reference to Jesus.

---

[22] Aloysius Pieris, *Fire & Water. Basic Issues in Asian Buddhism and Christianity*, chap. 17, 'The Spiritual Exercises on a Buddhist Background', previously published in *The Way Supplement* 68 (1990), 98–111.
[23] Ibid., p. 321.

This centrality is present in the prayers which are proper to each Week, and in the pathway presented by his life, passion, death and resurrection, as well as in the interlacing of specific Ignatian meditations: the Eternal King, the Two Standards and the Three Degrees of Humility. At first glance, therefore, this christocentrism is unavoidable. On the other hand, the opening (*Principle and Foundation*) and the conclusion (the *Contemplation for Attaining Love*) do not make it explicit. They do not do so because they begin from an interiorised christocentrism: they do not pray to Christ, but *from* Christ.

This gives us the clue to understand the absence of a divine Thou which we find above all in Zen. A *koan* proposes the following which, for Christian ears, is devastating: 'If you encounter the Buddha on the way, kill him'. Its meaning is that if you see a Buddha separate from yourself, it is not Buddha whom you see, but an image which you have created, still separate from you. Zen seeks to awake the Buddhistic nature of every person. Each one is the Buddha. Buddha does not exist separated from oneself. As long as it remains objectivised apart from the experience of the subject, there is distance and dualism. In the Christian experience, this can to some extent be parallel with the passage of the Ascension. The permanently visible presence of Christ would be an obstacle which we would have to overcome. 'It is for you that I go, because if I do not, the Paraclete could not come' (Jn 16:7). There is a time to be present and another time to be absent. It is on the basis of this rhythm of presences that we come increasingly towards him, and that we come to recognise that he remains at the base of who we are.

It is this which allows us to consider that there are diverse pathways to each momemt. It may happen that in a particular state of the spiritual way one may transcend the evangelical meditations, because the christological mediation has been interiorised. We are faced with an ancient polemic in the Church, which appears incidentally in the diverse hints of illuminism. It happened thus in the origins of the Society, when certain Jesuits opted for silent contemplative and unitive prayer – as opposed to mental and meditative – in the line of Carmelite prayer, and whom the first Fathers General held in suspicion.[24] St Teresa positioned herself before the danger of *iluminismo*, that is to say, of claiming a direct access to God without the mediation of the humanity of Jesus. (*Life* 22,1–10) On the other hand, a mystical tradition exists within the Church which harks back to Dionysius the Areopagite, continues in Meister Eckhart and in the anonymous English work *The Cloud of Unknowing*, arriving at St John of the Cross, which advocates contemplative prayer devoid of images and of all discursive activity, and which at no time ceases to be Christian.

f. In search of the Absolute

The three pathways offer the highest to which the human being can aspire, expressed according to the presuppositions of each tradition: the personal encounter with God through Jesus in the Exercises, absorption in the Ultimate Reality in Yoga, and the awakening to Pure Reality

---

[24] The Jesuits who were more inclined to mysticism were: Antonio Cordeses (1518–1601), Baltasar Álvarez (1535–1580), who was also confessor to Saint Teresa of Avila in his early years, and Álvarez de Paz (1560–1620), from Peru, who developed an important mystical theology: *De Inquisitione pacis* (1617). Cf. Philip Endean, "The Strange Style of Prayer", in The *Mercurian Project* (ed. Th. M. McCoog), Institutum Historicum Societatis Iesu (Rome) and The Institute of Jesuit Sources (St Louis), 2004, pp. 351–397. Also by Philip Endean: "The Original Line of Our Father Ignatius", op. cit., pp. 29–47.

in Zen. These ways are trusted, because through multiple generations they have proved capable of offering the necessary elements which lead to such peaks. Without this experience, there is no transformation. There has been an impoverishment of the Exercises when the ability to achieve such heights has been negated or held in suspicion, reducing them to a rationalistic method solely for discovering the will of God for one's own life, or a mere ethical action for making a permanent election. The mystical experience makes it possible for both things to be realised through God, and not through the resources of the ego. That which disposes 'for the way in which it could better serve God in the future' is precisely 'that the same Creator and Lord communicates himself to the devout soul, inflaming it with his love and praise'. (EE 15) It would be the experience of this embrace which best disposes it. This is implicitly through the First Time of Election: 'When God our Lord so moves and draws the will that, without doubting nor being able to doubt, the soul devotes itself to what it has been shown'. (EE 175) This movement and attraction are possible to the extent that the exercitant continues to evacuate the ego, just as he attempted to do in the First Week. As has been argued,[25] the consolation without previous cause is constitutive and not exceptional in the experience of the Exercises. Embrace, *extasis*, *samadhi*, *satori* ... these are terms to express the transforming experience of a dimension which is radical and absolute, in the roots and origins of our being, both in the ways of the West and of the East.

---

[25] Cf. José García de Castro, *El Dios emergente. La "consolación sin causa"*, Col. Manresa 26, Ed. Mensajero-Sal Terrae, 2002.

Conclusions

From the beginning of this study we have taken into account that each practice is linked to its original religious matrix. As we have said in the presentation, each spiritual way is the fruit as well as the seed of a way of conceiving of God, the human being and the world. Nevertheless, many masters of Yoga and Zen have insisted that they deal with practices independently of particular beliefs. Tiasen Deshimaru, one of the first masters to introduce Zen to the West, has said that 'Zen is beyond the religions.'[26] Illustrations of this are the diverse Christian authors who achieved remarkable syntheses and whose references we have included in the last part of the bibliography.

The specific value of the Exercises consists in their opening up to a radical otherness: Jesus Christ, which entails entering into the otherness of the other. This reflects its specific proposal: to sustain an election, a commitment, a concrete act of liberty in history. By contrast, Yoga and Zen enter into the non-temporality of the present moment, through non-discursivity, and seek reintegration into the primordial Unity, where God, world and humanity are one. The search for this silencing is the reason why there are increasing numbers of people practising Yoga or Zen. This shows the complementarity which exists between the distinct ways. Personalisation and trans-personalisation are the two poles of the human and religious experience. The first forms part of an essential moment of the psychological and spiritual experience: the consolidation of the 'I',

---

[26] Taisen Deshimaru, *Preguntas a un Maestro Zen*, Ed. Kairós, Barcelona, 1981, p. 7.

taking account of its irrepeatability. Insofar as the Ignatian Exercises are rooted in the Christian tradition, they foment the experience of a personal encounter with a personal God. Strengthened by the discernment of the election and the search for one's own vocation, the Ignatian way reinforces and expands the pole of personalisation. In times of searching and consolidation of one's own calling, the Exercises are the most opportune way. On the other hand, the trans-personal pole prevents the human from becoming the measure of all things, and this is what is distinctive about the oriental or oceanic religions, to which Yoga and Zen originally belonged.

From this we can investigate how both polarities are articulated, and to what extent the practices which spring from them can be compatible.

Yoga and Zen before the Exercises

Insofar as the first stages of the practice of Yoga and of Zen are physical-mental disciplines which place one in contact with the body and assist in the silencing of distractions of the mind, they can be considered as initial practices to prepare oneself for the experience of the Exercises. They propose a very suitable way towards interiorisation, and dispose the person to be *free from* the attachments of the ego. Once this liberty and this interior landscape have been achieved, one can undergo the experience of the Exercises which dispose one to be *free for* the discernment of a vocation and a mission. Both liberties (*free from* and *free for*) need and enrich one another. In other words, for many people, the practice of Yoga or Zen can be the way to an interiority which they could not attain by means of Christian practices. Once the access to the interior world is open, the gospels and the person of Jesus acquire a resonance they did not have before;

this makes favourable an experience of the Exercises which was otherwise blocked off. It is increasingly common to meet people who have come to make the Exercises after having made this detour to the East. They explain that they have rediscovered the interiority of Christianity thanks to the practices of these other traditions.

YOGA AND ZEN AFTER THE EXERCISES

But the practice of Yoga or Zen cannot only be situated before, but can also recover – or begin – as a result of an experience of the Exercises. Once the election is made and the personal vocation discovered, the oriental ways lead into the transpersonal ambit. Transpersonalisation is alien neither to Christianity nor to the Exercises, insofar as, through the election, the exercitant has to enter into the Third and Fourth Weeks, where the same person of Jesus is found on transpersonal coordinates. Frequently it is not known how to accompany such an experience; usually the passages of the appearances of the Risen Christ are treated according to the key of the Second Week, without the exercitant having truly handed over and transcended the 'I', which is the distinctive feature of the last two weeks: the Third Week as kenosis and the Fourth as plenitude. This explains why the horizon of the *Contemplation for Attaining Love* is rarely achieved. The majority of exercitants remain on the threshold. In this sense, we may say with Hugo Enomiya-Lasalle that 'where the Exercises finish, *zazen* begins'[27] just as the advanced practice of yoga is the key of *advaita* or non-duality.

---

[27] *Zazen y los Ejercicios de San Ignacio* (1975), Ed. Paulinas, 1985, p. 43.

Towards Possible Syntheses

The three ways are endorsed by many masters and generations of practitioners who have given them a vote of confidence. Each one has its own coherence and only advances if one hands oneself over, and if there is a deep trust in the practice which is being proposed. If this is so, then in principle it is not necessary to incorporate heterogeneous elements, nor is it illegitimate to consider to what point each way may be enriched with complementary elements, without them losing their unique identity. To be open to other practices which observe the same peaks requires receptivity and lucidity: lucidity so as to avoid the self-deceptions which pester the regions of every ascent, as well as to allow for enriching syntheses which are not toxic mixtures.

The essence of Christianity is that God has revealed himself in the Face of Jesus Christ, and the Exercises revolve around the contemplation of this Face, a face which each exercitant has to recreate in his life and discover in the history of his contemporaries. The christification is happening to the extent that, in conceiving of one's life as a vocation and a mission, the person is achieving fullness in tune with the evacuation of his self-offering. For this reason it can be opportune to introduce corporal and respiratory practices which arrest mental activity and favour the difficult dis-identification with the ego. In the same way, one may favour approximation to those regions in which everything becomes transparent, and where the 'I' does not remain in the self, but is a receptacle of the Whole and of everything which transcends it.

These pages have not been able to resolve many questions which still remain, but perhaps have been able to give some clues to indicate integrations we have scarcely begun to recognise. Through the search for the spiritual experience and the opening to the Real which is a given among our contemporaries, we are called to let ourselves be interrogated and enriched by the contributions of other religious traditions. Because all originate in the same Fount and return to it, through the same paradoxes of God or of the Ultimate Reality: fullness spills out into donation.

FURTHER READING

SOURCES

Ignatius of Loyola, *Spiritual Exercises*, in *Personal Writings*, Penguin Books, London.

Hinduism
Bhagavad Gita, Penguin Books, London.
Pantanjali, *Yoga Sutras,* HarperCollins Publishers India, New Delhi.
The Principal Upanishads (ed. by S. Radhakrishna), HarperCollins Publishers India, New Delhi.

Zen
Cleary, Th., (ed.), *Zen Essence. The Classic Texts of the Chinese Masters*, Shambala Editions, Berkeley, 2000.

STUDIES

Bauberger, Stefan, 'Ignatian Spirituality and the Practice of Zen', *Ignis* 28 (1999), pp. 62–69.
Dumoulin, Heinrich, *Christianity Meets Buddhism*, La Salle, Illinois, 1974.
Eliade, Mircea, *Yoga, Immortality and Freedom* (1954), Princeton Univ. Press, 1973.
Enomiya-Lassalle, Hugo, *The Practice of Zen Meditation*, HarperCollins, New York, 1987.
Habito, Ruben, *Living Zen, Loving God*, Wisdom Publications, 2004.
Hand, Thomas & Lee, Chwen Jiuan A., *A Taste of Water*, Paulist Press, Mahwah, New Jersey, 1990.
Herrigel, Eugen, *Zen in the Art of Archery*, Penguin, New York, 1988.

Johnston, William, *The Still Point, Reflections on Zen and Christian Mystics,* Fordham University Press, New York, 1970.

Johnston, William, *Christian Zen: A Way of Meditation,* Harper Row, New York, 1981.

Kadowaki, J. K., *Zen and the Bible,* Routledge & Kegan Paul, New York, 1980.

Malpan, Varguese, *A Comparative Study of the Bhagavad Gita and the Spiritual Exercises of Saint Ignatius of Loyola on the Process of Spiritual Liberation,* Editrice Pont. Univ. Gregoriana, Roma, 1992.

Mann, Thomas, *Zen and the Birds of Appetite* (1968).

Mello, Anthony de, *Sadhana: A Way to God,* Doubleday, New York, 1984.

Nishitani, Keiji, *Religion and Nothingness* (1982).

O'Hanlon, Daniel, 'Zen and the Spiritual Exercises: A Dialogue Between Faiths', *Theological Studies,* Vol. 39, No. 4, Dec. 1978.

Painadath, Sebastian, SJ, 'The Integrated Spirituality of the Bhagavad Gita – An Insight for Christians: A Contribution to the Hindu-Christian Dialogue', *Journal of Ecumenical Studies,* Vol. 39, 2002.

Pieris, Aloysius, *Fire & Water. Basic Issues in Asian Buddhism and Christianity,* chap.17, "The Spiritual Exercises on a Buddhist Background", previously published in *The Way Supplement* 68 (1990), 98–111.

Senecal, Bernard, 'Zen et Exercices spirituels', *Christus* 162 (1994); "Zen y Ejercicios Espirituales", Diccionario de Espiritualidad Ignaciana, II, Mensajero-Sal Terrae, Bilbao-Santander, 2007, p. 1798.

Zuzuki, D. T., *Essays in Zen Buddhism,* Rider & Co., London, 1970, Vol. I–III.

www.ingramcontent.com/pod-product-compliance
Lightning Source LLC
Chambersburg PA
CBHW020020050426
42450CB00005B/564